I SPY

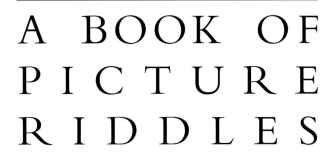

YEAR-ROUND CHALLENGER!

A BOOK OF PICTURE RIDDLES

Photographs by Walter Wick

Riddles by Jean Marzollo

Cartwheel B·O·O·K·S ®

SCHOLASTIC INC.

New York   Toronto   London   Auckland   Sydney
Mexico City   New Delhi   Hong Kong   Buenos Aires

For Michaela and Jonathan Slavid
and Allegra and Olivia Cords

———

W.W.

To the Rural & Migrant Ministry
Hope, Justice, & Empowerment

———

J.M.

Book design by Carol Devine Carson

Go to www.scholastic.com for Web site information
on Scholastic authors and illustrators.

"Bulletin Board" and "At the Beach" from *I Spy* © 1992 by Walter Wick; "The Holly and the Ivy" and
"Window Shopping" from *I Spy Christmas* © 1992 by Walter Wick; "Prizes to Win" from *I Spy Fun House*
© 1993 by Walter Wick; "Mystery by the Sea" from *I Spy Mystery* © 1993 by Walter Wick; "Into the Woods"
from *I Spy Fantasy* © 1994 by Walter Wick; "Be My Valentine," "Stegosaurus," "Chalkboard Fun," and
"Nature Close Up" from *I Spy School Days* © 1995 by Walter Wick; "House on the Hill" from *I Spy Spooky
Night* © 1996 by Walter Wick. All published by Scholastic Inc.

Library of Congress Cataloging-in-Publication Data available

Reinforced Library Edition
ISBN-13: 978-0-439-68433-0
ISBN-10: 0-439-68433-1

10 9 8 7 6 5   8 9 10 11/0

Printed in Malaysia   46
This edition, March 2005

TABLE OF CONTENTS

Picture riddles fill this book;
Turn the pages! Take a look!

Use your mind, use your eye;
Read the riddles—play I SPY!

I spy three walnuts, four almonds, four bows,
Two shiny gold stars, and an elfin nose;

A button, a book, a band of lace,
A bear sextet, and a white mustache face.

I spy SUNSHINE, an envelope for Sam,
A mailbox flag, a piggy bank, a lamb;

A king, a queen, a ring, a dove,
A smiling house, and an astronaut in love.

11

The Stegosaurus ate plants for food. Bobby C.

Stegosaurus walks on four legs and is my favorite dinosaur. Rosa

Nobody knows what they are really like because they only have the bones.

This shows how big a Stegosaurus is compared to a school bus. Joel

SCHOOL BUS

Stegosaurus' brain was only as big as a walnut.

Stegosaurus' tail spikes could b

I spy four crayons, a paper cup display,

Three people, a sun, and the U.S.A.;

Brian J.
I like the stegasaurus because it has spikes on its tail.
carrie
Stegosaurus babies were hatched from eggs like reptiles.
CANADA
Wyoming
Utah
Colorado
Oklahoma
Mexico
Stars show where Stegosduruses were found. Toby
A Dinosaur Dig
Fossils show what the bones were like. Paleontologists are the people who like to dig them out of the rocks and study them. Roberto
s long as a yard stick.
Book of Dinosaur FACTS
by

A paintbrush, a paper clip, a triceratops,
Four bobby pins, and four bloody drops.

I spy three clothespins, a rain hat and coat,

Three horses, three hearts, and a peaceful sailboat;

A skier, a biker, four buttons, a skate,
Four dogs, four cats, and a white license plate.

I spy a wheelbarrow, a January bear,
A birdhouse, a bugle, and a folding chair;

Two tubas, three arrows, a heart, a dish,
A frying pan, a fox, and two unlucky fish.

I spy two beach balls, four shovels, a chick,

A funnel, an ant, and a sandy craft stick;

Three flags, a flamingo, a surfin' fella,
A small steering wheel, and a fancy umbrella.

I spy a hammer, a golf tee, a bat,

Four button holes, and a dark top hat;

A corncob, a feather, a small soccer ball,
A safety pin, a bike, and seven bears in all.

I spy three bottles, two starfish, a string,
A poodle, a pearl, a leaf, and a ring;

Four feathers, a button, a cork, a key,
A turtle, a coin, a 4, and a B.

I spy twelve arrows, two squares to be blue,
An exclamation point, two gerbils, a Q;

Two erasers, a bird, a yellow three,
Two question marks, and a pink apostrophe.

I spy eight flowerpots, a sign on a bone,

A pitchfork, a cage, and an old gramophone;

A rabbit, an octagon, six pin stripes, a 4,
A candelabra, a hanger, and a dollhouse door.

I spy a pencil, four blueberries, a bee,
And a winged pair of seeds from a maple tree;

The word IN twice, a bottle cap, a pin,
Two sunflower seeds, and a piece of snakeskin.

29

I spy a gas pump and Santa's green sack,

A football, hinged knees, and a milk bottle stack;

A caboose, a teacup, a domino, a deer,
And a band to celebrate the end of the year!

EXTRA CREDIT RIDDLES

Find the Pictures That Go with These Riddles:

I spy two anchors, two slides, orange string,

A soda can, JAMAICA, a fence, and SPRING.

I spy a road sign, a yellow car,

Three paper clips, a harp, and a shadowy star.

I spy a chair, a bird in a tree,

A watering can, a pitcher, and a 3.

I spy some whiskers, a clock, a balloon,

A place to be red, a magnet, and a moon.

I spy an accordion, a small scarf of blue,

A white bird, a chain, and a red beak, too.

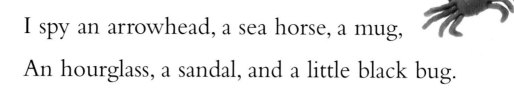

I spy an arrowhead, a sea horse, a mug,

An hourglass, a sandal, and a little black bug.

I spy a fern, two fall leaves of red,

Clover, a five, and a president's head.

I spy a lobster, a little seventeen,

A Ferris wheel, an ant, and a sweet jellybean.

I spy two alligators, a yardstick, a bus,

A little black lizard, and a purple stegosaurus.

I spy a turtle, a whistle, a bear,

A snorkel, GULL, and a flipper pair.

I spy two trunks, a lion's mane,

A tambourine, and a candy cane.

I spy a squirrel, a lizard on a log,

A sax, a drum, and a golfing frog.

About the Creators of *I Spy*

Jean Marzollo has written many award-winning children's books, including twelve I Spy books and seven I Spy Little books. She has also written: *I Love You: A Rebus Poem*, illustrated by Suse MacDonald; *I Am Planet Earth*, illustrated by Judith Moffatt; *Happy Birthday, Martin Luther King*, illustrated by Brian Pinkney; *Thanksgiving Cats*, illustrated by Hans Wilhelm; *Shanna's Princess Show* and *Shanna's Doctor Show*, illustrated by Shane W. Evans; *Pretend You're a Cat*, illustrated by Jerry Pinkney; *Mama Mama*, illustrated by Laura Regan; *Home Sweet Home*, illustrated by Ashley Wolff; *Soccer Sam*, illustrated by Blanche Sims; and *Close Your Eyes*, illustrated by Susan Jeffers. For nineteen years, Jean Marzollo and Carol Carson produced Scholastic's kindergarten magazine, *Let's Find Out*. Ms. Marzollo holds a master's degree from the Harvard Graduate School of Education. She is the 2000 recipient of the Rip Van Winkle Award presented by the School Library Media Specialists of Southeastern New York. She lives with her husband, Claudio, in New York State's Hudson Valley.

Walter Wick is the photographer of the I Spy books. He is author and photographer of *A Drop of Water: A Book of Science and Wonder*, which won the Boston Globe/Horn Book Award for Nonfiction, was named a Notable Children's Book by the American Library Association, and was selected as an Orbis Pictus Honor Book and a CBC/NSTA Outstanding Science Trade Book for Children. *Walter Wick's Optical Tricks*, a book of photographic illusions, was named a Best Illustrated Children's Book by *The New York Times Book Review*, was recognized as a Notable Children's Book by the American Library Association, and received many awards, including a Platinum Award from the Oppenheim Toy Portfolio, a Young Readers Award from *Scientific American*, a *Bulletin* Blue Ribbon, and a Parents' Choice Silver Honor. Mr. Wick has invented photographic games for *Games* magazine and photographed covers for books and magazines, including *Newsweek*, *Discover*, and *Psychology Today*. A graduate of Paier College of Art, Mr. Wick lives with his wife, Linda, in New York and Connecticut.

Carol Devine Carson, the book designer for the I Spy series, is the art director for a major publishing house in New York City.

Catch the I Spy Spirit!

Catch the I Spy spirit, and create your own I Spy pictures and riddles. To make the pictures, first study the photos in the book. Think about how the pictures were created before they were photographed. Then think of how you want to make your picture. Maybe you want to construct something or lay out objects on a table. Perhaps you'd rather draw objects, cut out pictures from a magazine, and/or use stickers to make your picture. Use your imagination!

To write your own riddle rhymes, read aloud the riddles in this book. Can you hear the pattern of the rhythm? It's a 3/4 waltz rhythm: 1-2-3, 1-2-3, 1-2-3, 1-2-3. There are four main beats to a line. You can sing all the I Spy riddles to an old-fashioned song called *Sweet Betsy from Pike*. Ask your music teacher to help you learn the song. Interestingly, rap also has four main beats to a line. Many children today find it helpful to rap the I Spy riddles in order to understand the rhythmic pattern. Notice, also, the rhyme scheme for I Spy. The first two lines rhyme, and the last two lines rhyme. Tip #1: Write your riddles before or while you're making your picture. That way you can be sure to have the rhyming words you need. Tip #2: Take your time. Creating I Spy pictures may be more challenging than you think!

The Story of *I Spy Year-Round Challenger!*

The I Spy Challenger books have been created in response to those children who have found every single thing in every I Spy book, including items listed in the Extra Credit Riddles. These kids demand harder riddles and often suggest themes. This time we have responded to requests for a type of calendar book with pictures for every month. Kids always ask: "What's the hardest thing to find?" In this book, it seems to be the queen in February's photo. Will it take you a year to find?

Acknowledgments

We would like to thank the following hard-working members of Girl Scout Troop 1405 for testing the riddles in this book: Cassie Barcavage, Jennifer Cotennec, Michelle Cotennec, Danielle Etta, Rachel Flaherty, Katie McConville, Kelly O'Campo, Faye Rice, Meghan Spratt, Megan Volkmann, Elizabeth Wilcox, and Emily Young, as well as their dynamic troop leader, Donna Cotennec. Once again, we'd like to extend thanks to David Marzollo for his superlative creative advice and excellent I Spy eyes.

Jean Marzollo and Walter Wick

I Spy Books for All Ages:
I SPY: A BOOK OF PICTURE RIDDLES
I SPY CHRISTMAS
I SPY EXTREME CHALLENGER!
I SPY FANTASY
I SPY FUN HOUSE
I SPY GOLD CHALLENGER!
I SPY MYSTERY
I SPY SCHOOL DAYS
I SPY SPOOKY NIGHT
I SPY SUPER CHALLENGER!
I SPY TREASURE HUNT
I SPY ULTIMATE CHALLENGER!
I SPY YEAR-ROUND CHALLENGER!

Books for New Readers:
SCHOLASTIC READER LVL 1: I SPY A BALLOON
SCHOLASTIC READER LVL 1: I SPY A BUTTERFLY
SCHOLASTIC READER LVL 1: I SPY A CANDY CANE
SCHOLASTIC READER LVL 1: I SPY A DINOSAUR'S EYE
SCHOLASTIC READER LVL 1: I SPY A PENGUIN
SCHOLASTIC READER LVL 1: I SPY A PUMPKIN
SCHOLASTIC READER LVL 1: I SPY A SCARY MONSTER
SCHOLASTIC READER LVL 1: I SPY A SCHOOL BUS
SCHOLASTIC READER LVL 1: I SPY FUNNY TEETH
SCHOLASTIC READER LVL 1: I SPY LIGHTNING IN THE SKY
SCHOLASTIC READER LVL 1: I SPY SANTA CLAUS

And for the Youngest Child:
I SPY LITTLE ANIMALS
I SPY LITTLE BOOK
I SPY LITTLE BUNNIES
I SPY LITTLE CHRISTMAS
I SPY LITTLE LEARNING BOX
I SPY LITTLE LETTERS
I SPY LITTLE NUMBERS
I SPY LITTLE WHEELS

Also Available:
I SPY CHALLENGER FOR GAME BOY ADVANCE
I SPY JUNIOR: PUPPET PLAYHOUSE CD-ROM
I SPY JUNIOR CD-ROM
I SPY SCHOOL DAYS CD-ROM
I SPY SPOOKY MANSION CD-ROM
I SPY TREASURE HUNT CD-ROM

Reviews and Praise for I Spy

For *I Spy Treasure Hunt:*

Marzollo's structured rhymes provide the clues while Wick's stunningly detailed miniature village provides the hidden answers for readers to seek out.

School Library Journal

For *I Spy Gold Challenger!:*

The I Spy concept is a deceptively simple one — look for particular items in meticulously arranged photos that are often startling in their artistry.

The Hamilton Spectator

For *I Spy Super Challenger!:*

The trademark rhyming riddles lead sharp-eyed readers to objects in crisp photographs. Wick's painstakingly prepared illustrations — bright, elaborate, and wonderfully thematic — strike a great balance between shape and color.

Booklist

For the Educational Value of the I Spy Books:

Kids find I Spy engaging because it builds on their excellent visual discrimination skills. It also challenges them incrementally with some initial success virtually guaranteed. Good teachers provide for instruction this way — and it works! Another appeal of I Spy, besides the sheer beauty of Walter Wick's photographs, is their uniqueness. They capture our attention because they are different and interesting. Brain research tells us that learners respond to novelty. As children respond to I Spy, they improve their reading, writing, rhyming, critical thinking, and vocabulary skills.

Dr. Joanne Marien,
Assistant Superintendent
Curriculum and Instruction
Somers Public Schools
Somers, NY